Copyright © 2023 Hayde Miller
All rights reserved. This book or any portion thereof may not be reproduced or used in any manner whatsoever without the express written permission of the publisher except for the use of brief quotations in a book review.

Day by Day Affirmations journal

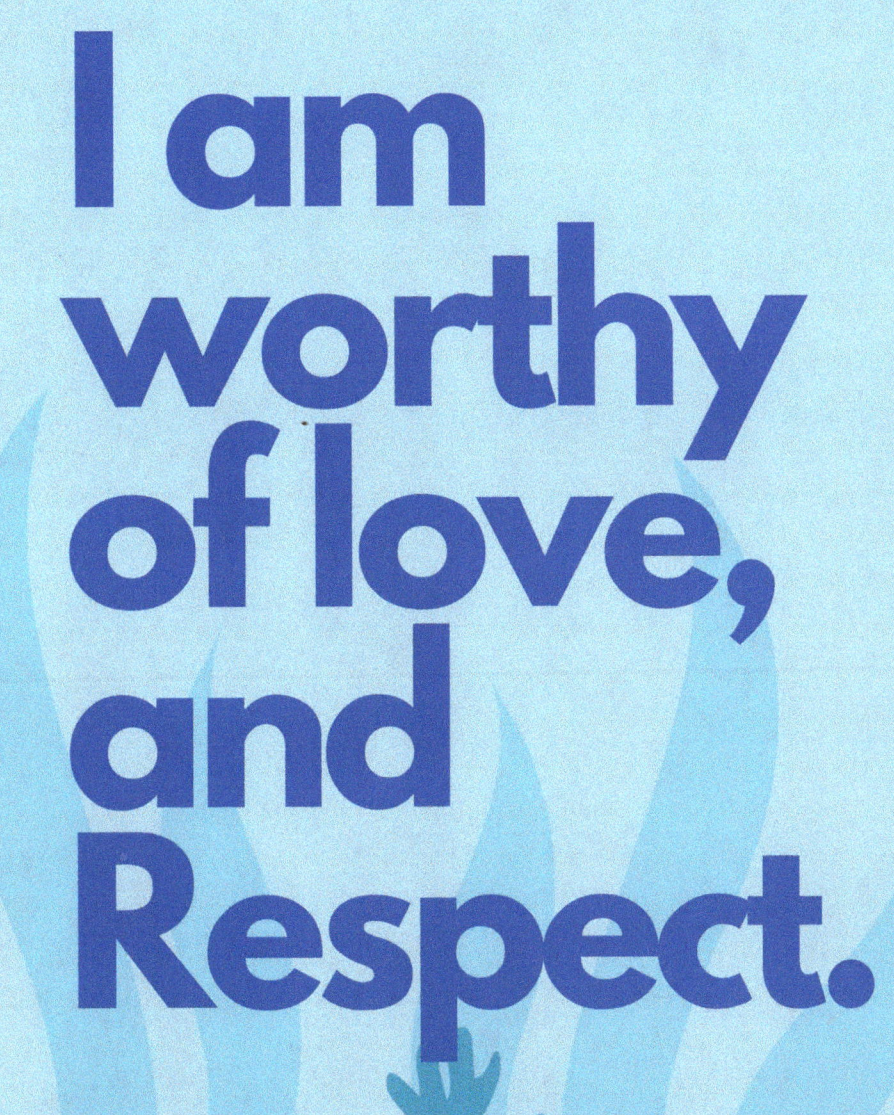

Daily Notes

I love myself Unconditionally.

Daily Notes

I am Strong, and Capable.

Daily Notes

I am surrounded by love.

Daily Notes

I am open to giving, and receiving love.

Daily Notes

I am worthy of living a life of joy, and abundance

Daily Notes

I am grateful for the love that I have to give.

Daily Notes

I am capable of achieving anything I set my mind to.

Daily Notes

I am worthy of all good things life has to offer.

Daily Notes

I am
open
to new
opportunities,
and
experiences.

Daily Notes

I am grateful for all that I have, and all that I am.

Daily Notes

I am taking steps towards creating a life I love.

Daily Notes

I am worthy of pursing my dreams, and creating the life I desire.

Daily Notes

I am worthy of love, and Happiness

Daily Notes

Daily Notes

I am worthy of success and abundance

Daily Notes

I choose to focus on the positives in my life, and be thankful for them.

Daily Notes

I am capable of overcoming any challenge that comes my way.

Daily Notes

Daily Notes

I will look for the good in every situation.

Daily Notes

Daily Notes

I will stay Focused on my faith goals.

Daily Notes

I have the power to create the life I desire.

Daily Notes

I am blessed and highly favored.

Daily Notes

I will be patient, and practice Self-compassion

Daily Notes

I will listen to my intutition, and trust my inner wisdom.

Daily Notes

I am grateful for the relationships I have in my life.

Daily Notes

I am grateful for God's unconditional love.

Daily Notes

I am beautiful inside and out.

Daily Notes

I can be anything.

Daily Notes

Daily Notes

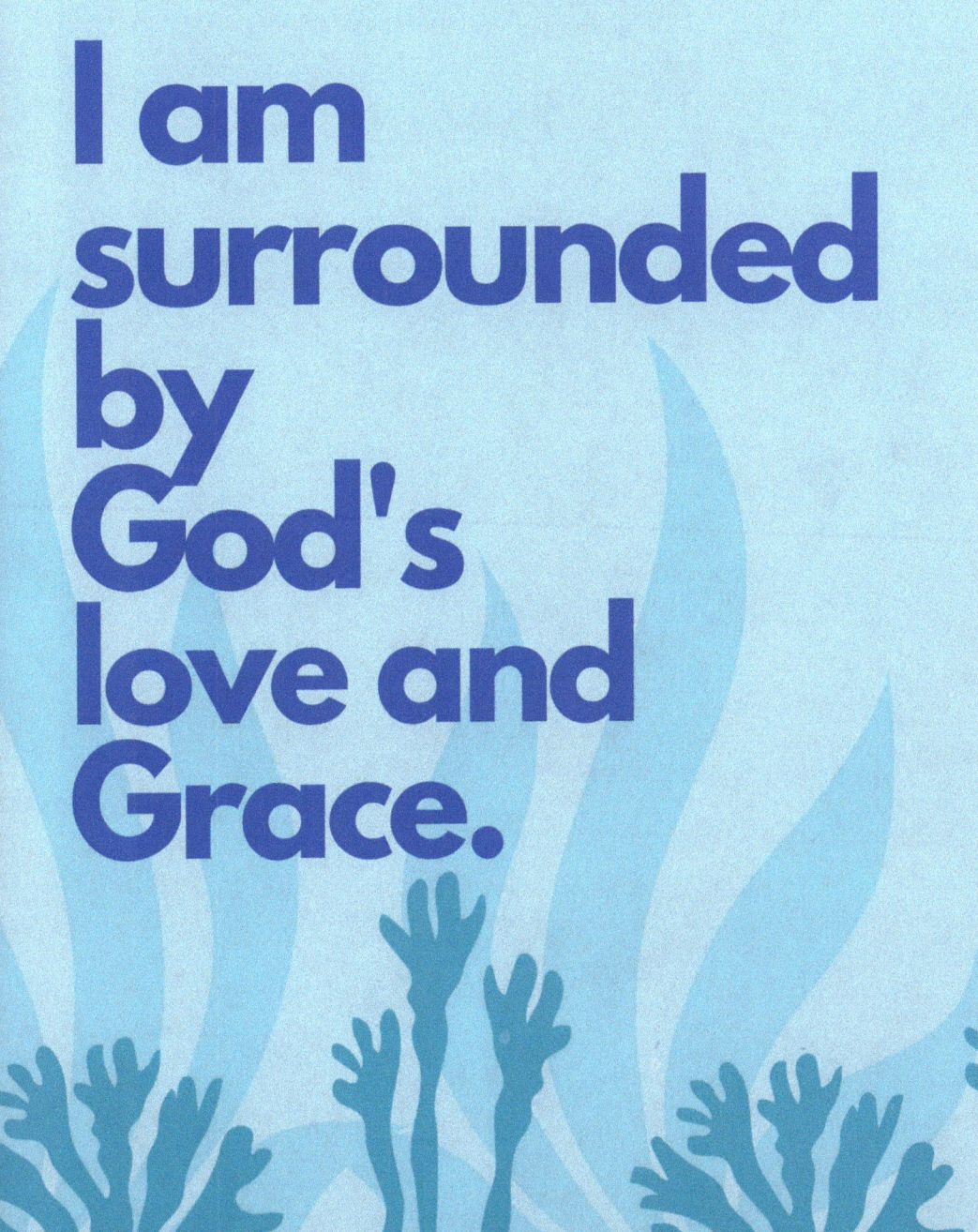

Daily Notes

I will be happy and face all my fears.

Daily Notes

I will see the best in myself and learn to improve.

Daily Notes

Daily Notes

I will be motivated today and everyday.

Daily Notes

It's ok to not be ok.

www.ingramcontent.com/pod-product-compliance
Lightning Source LLC
Chambersburg PA
CBHW070208100426
42743CB00013B/3103